EVANS V.
WASHINGTONIA STATE UNIVERSITY

EVANS V. WASHINGTONIA STATE UNIVERSITY

Elizabeth L. Lippy

Partner, Fairlie & Lippy, P.C.
Assistant Director of Trial Advocacy
American University Washington College of Law

NATIONAL INSTITUTE FOR TRIAL ADVOCACY

Address inquiries to:
Reprint Permission
National Institute for Trial Advocacy
1685 38th Street, Suite 200
Boulder, CO 80301-2735
Phone: (800) 225-6482
Fax: (720) 890-7069
E-mail: permissions@nita.org

ISBN 978-1-60156-398-9
FBA 1398

14 13 12 11 10 9 8 7 6 5 4 3 2 1

Printed in the United States of America

ACKNOWLEDGMENTS

I would like to acknowledge the special contributions made by current and former students of the American University Washington College of Law (WCL) who helped research, draft, and edit this case file, particularly Allyson Breech, Ryan Norman, Brittany Gail Thomas, and Annie Berry.

Thanks also to my colleague and NITA author Liz Boals, associate director of the WCL Trial Advocacy Program, for always providing a second look and a detailed edit. To Kim Green, program coordinator, and Mary Ippolito, senior administrative assistant, at WCL for their constant support and help.

I couldn't be doing what I do without the help and support of my law partner, Steven F. Fairlie, who somehow lets me be in two places at once.

Last but not least, my modern family and my true partner, my amazing husband . . . without whom I could not accomplish half of my goals.

Liz Lippy
January 2014

The National Institute for Trial Advocacy wishes to thank Facebook for its permission to use likenesses of its website as part of these teaching materials.

CONTENTS

CASE SUMMARY

This is a civil action for negligence brought by the plaintiff Riley Evans against the defendant Washingtonia State University. Evans alleges that Washingtonia State University, in violation of the Washingtonia School Cyberbullying Protection Act ("CBPA") and university policy, failed to provide a safe learning environment and did not prevent hostile cyberbullying that substantially interfered with Evans's education.

In Fall YR-3, Riley Evans was a student at Washingtonia State University and was enrolled in a popular course entitled Politics and Social Media, taught by Adjunct Professor Jamie Winstone. The course, designed to teach students about the role of the Internet and social media in political campaigns, involved students running simulated presidential campaigns using social websites such as Facebook. Evans and one other student, Morgan Ritchfield, were selected by Winstone to be the presidential candidates in the class. The remaining students were split into two groups and assigned to help run the candidates' campaigns.

Morgan Ritchfield and students from the opposing campaign team began posting material about Evans on a Facebook page entitled Politics and Social Media YR-3 Election, stating that Evans was known to have cheated in an unrelated class, made fun of a disabled student, and was seen drinking underage at a campus fraternity party and included a video of the alleged incident. Evans notified Winstone on two occasions about the nature of the posts on Facebook, but Winstone failed to do anything about them. Winstone replied that the posts were nothing more than hard-nosed campaigning and typical campaign mudslinging.

Following the Facebook posts, Evans was investigated by the Washingtonia State University Academic Integrity Board and received a summons to report to the board for a hearing on information involving allegations of cheating and underage drinking. However, Evans withdrew from the university before the hearing could take place.

The applicable law is contained in the statutes and proposed jury instructions set forth at the end of this case file. All years in these materials are stated in the following form:

YR-0 indicates the actual year in which the case is being tried (i.e., the present year);

YR-1 indicates the preceding year (please use the actual year);

YR-2 indicates the next preceding year (please use the actual year); et cetera.

SPECIAL INSTRUCTIONS FOR USE AS A FULL TRIAL

When this case file is used for a full trial, the following witnesses may be called by the parties:

Plaintiff: Riley Evans

                     Jamie Winstone

Defendant: Morgan Ritchfield

                     Dylan Jeffries

All witnesses are gender neutral and may be either male or female.

Limitation on Witnesses:

Each party is limited to two witnesses.

Required Stipulations:

1.   Federal Rules of Civil Procedure and Federal Rules of Evidence apply.

2.   All witnesses called to testify who have identified the parties, other individuals, or tangible evidence in depositions or prior testimony can and will, if asked, identify the same at trial.

3.   Each witness who gave a deposition agreed under oath at the outset of his or her testimony to give a full and complete description of all material events that occurred and to correct the transcript of such deposition or testimony for inaccuracies and completeness before signing the transcript.

4.   All depositions and transcripts of testimony were signed under oath.

5.   The plaintiff and the defendant must call the two witnesses listed as that party's witnesses on the witness list.

6.   All exhibits in the file are authentic. In addition, each exhibit contained in the file is the original of that document unless otherwise noted on the exhibit or as established by the evidence.

7.   This case comes to trial in YR-2.

8.   The defendant attempted to file a cross-complaint against Adjunct Professor Jamie Winstone. However, the judge ruled that the immunity clause of the State of Washingtonia School Cyberbullying Protection Act of YR-6 protected Winstone from any such suit.

9.   The defendant filed a cross-complaint against Morgan Ritchfield. A confidential settlement occurred and may not be mentioned before the jury.

10. The Facebook page entitled Politics and Social Media YR-3 Election can be found at http://bit.ly/1frS1BM.

11. Exhibit 9 is a screenshot of the Facebook page entitled Politics and Social Media YR-3 Election, and reflects all posts made on the page. Seventy-six people with Facebook profiles became members of the page during the Fall YR-3 semester. The only administrator of the page was the course instructor, Adjunct Professor Jamie Winstone. The Facebook page was capable of being downloaded and disseminated electronically.

12. The individual profile pages for Morganmaniac, Mritch4prez, EvansYR-3, Goldiephd, Morgan Ritchfield, RitchfieldYR-3, Evanslvr, and Jamie Winstone are inaccessible.

13. Counsel for the plaintiff sent a request to defense counsel on November 4, YR-3, requesting that the Facebook page not be altered, destroyed, or modified in any way. Defense complied with the request, and the Facebook page has not been altered from the date of the last posting, November 3, YR-3. Further, the Facebook page was no longer "live" on the Internet as of November 4, YR-3.

14. Adjunct professors, adjunct faculty, and any deans at state-funded universities are considered agents of the state-funded university. *See Machovina v. Washingtonia State University*, 99 W.S.2d 1250 (Washingtonia YR-4).

15. Exhibit 13 is a screenshot of student evaluations of Professor Jamie Winstone from the website TeacherMeter (http://bit.ly/1jCxdNz) in August YR-3.

16. This is a bifurcated trial. At this point in the trial, the jury is only deciding whether Washingtonia State University was negligent or whether Riley Evans assumed the risk.

BREECH & BREECH, PC

Attorney ID # 24601

EBreech@bbpc.nita

1501 Tort State Road

Rightsville, Washingtonia 01234

ATTORNEY FOR PLAINTIFF

DISTRICT COURT OF THE STATE OF NITA — CIVIL DIVISION

RILEY EVANS	:	No. 123-YR-2
v.	:	
WASHINGTONIA STATE UNIVERSITY	:	

<u>NOTICE</u>

You have been sued in court. If you wish to defend against the claims set forth in the following pages, you must take action within twenty days after this complaint and notice are served by entering a written appearance personally, or by an attorney, to the claims set forth against you. You are warned that if you fail to do so, the case may proceed without you and a judgment may be entered against you by the court, without further claims or relief requested by the plaintiff. You may lose money, property, or other rights important to you.

BREECH & BREECH, PC

Attorney ID # 24601

EBreech@bbpc.nita

1501 Tort State Road

Rightsville, Washingtonia 01234

ATTORNEY FOR PLAINTIFF

DISTRICT COURT OF THE STATE OF NITA — CIVIL DIVISION

RILEY EVANS	:	No. 123-YR-2
v.	:	
WASHINGTONIA STATE UNIVERSITY	:	

COMPLAINT

The plaintiff, by and through undersigned counsel, brings this action at law and respectfully represents:

1. The plaintiff, Riley Evans, is an adult individual with a permanent address of 200 West Oxfield Lane, Oaksville, Washingtonia.

2. The defendant, Washingtonia State University, is a quasi-municipal corporation created pursuant to the laws of the State of Washingtonia and is controlled by state guidelines of Washingtonia and as such is governed by the Washingtonia School Cyberbullying Protection Act ("CBPA").

3. Venue and jurisdiction in this court is proper, as the plaintiff is a resident of Washingtonia and all facilities of the Washingtonia State University are located in this judicial district.

4. In or about August YR-4, the plaintiff enrolled as a student at the Washingtonia State University and was so enrolled during the YR-3/YR-2 academic year.

5. In or about August YR-3, the plaintiff was a sophomore at Washingtonia State University and enrolled in a course entitled Politics and Social Media, which was offered at the school for the two prior academic years and was taught by Adjunct Professor Jamie Winstone (hereinafter "Professor Winstone").

6. During the Fall YR-3 semester, the students in Politics and Social Media engaged in a mock presidential election and campaign utilizing social media, which included Facebook.

7. As part of the aforementioned assignment, Professor Winstone appointed two students as the presidential candidates—specifically, the plaintiff and another sophomore student named Morgan Ritchfield.

8. During the presidential election campaign process in Politics and Social Media, the plaintiff became the subject of cyberbullying by students at Washingtonia State University including, but not limited to, taunting, teasing, and bullying through the Internet (hereinafter "cyberbullying") to such a degree that the plaintiff became anxious, upset, depressed, and socially withdrawn and the cyberbullying substantially interfered with the plaintiff's educational experience.

COUNT I — NEGLIGENCE

9. The plaintiff hereby incorporates by reference the averments set forth in Paragraphs 1 through 8 as though fully set forth herein at length.

10. At all relevant times, the defendant owed a duty to provide a safe and appropriate environment for the plaintiff to learn and benefit from the education provided by Washingtonia State University and to prevent a hostile environment that substantially interfered with the plaintiff's education performance, opportunities, or benefits, in accordance with the Washingtonia School Cyberbullying Protection Act, 18 W.C.L. § 3952(b) ("CBPA").

11. The plaintiff had multiple meetings with Professor Winstone regarding the cyberbullying and therefore the defendant was on notice that the plaintiff was a target of the ongoing abuse.

12. Despite the plaintiff's regular and repeated requests for help, the defendant consistently failed to prevent the ongoing abuse or to take any meaningful measures to prevent the ongoing cyberbullying.

13. As a result of the defendant's utter failure to act in spite of notice, and as a result of the ongoing cyberbullying, the plaintiff withdrew as a student at Washingtonia State University on November 3, YR-3.

14. As a direct and proximate cause of the actions and/or omissions of Defendant, the plaintiff suffered, among other things, emotional distress.

15. The plaintiff is entitled to recover damages, which the plaintiff claims in excess of FIFTY THOUSAND ($50,000.00) DOLLARS together with costs, interest, and attorney fees as allowed by law.

WHEREFORE, the plaintiff respectfully requests judgment against the Washingtonia State University in an amount yet to be determined, including reasonable attorney fees and costs.

Respectfully submitted,

BREECH & BREECH, PC

By: _____*E. Breech*_____
Attorney for Plaintiff

VERIFICATION

I, Riley Evans, am the plaintiff in the within action and state that the facts set forth in the foregoing complaint are true, correct, and accurate to the best of my information and belief. I understand that false statements made herein are subject to penalty of law relating unsworn falsifications to authorities.

Riley Evans
_____
Riley Evans, plaintiff   January 10, YR-2

DEFENSE ATTORNEYS, LTD.

Attorney ID # 66612

Jnucci@daltd.nita

4 Defense Road

Rightsville, Washingtonia 01233

ATTORNEY FOR DEFENDANT

DISTRICT COURT OF THE STATE OF NITA — CIVIL DIVISION

RILEY EVANS   :   No. 123-YR-2

v.   :

WASHINGTONIA STATE UNIVERSITY   :

<u>ANSWER</u>

The defendant, Washingtonia State University, by and through undersigned counsel, hereby answers the plaintiff's complaint and respectfully represents:

1. Admitted.

2. Admitted.

3. Admitted.

4. Admitted.

5. Admitted.

6. Admitted.

7. Denied. It is specifically denied that Professor Winstone appointed the plaintiff as the presidential candidate. To the contrary, the plaintiff volunteered to become the presidential candidate and was only appointed to that position after the plaintiff volunteered.

8. Denied. It is specifically denied that the plaintiff became the subject of cyberbullying by students at Washingtonia State University, that the plaintiff became anxious, upset, depressed, and socially withdrawn, and that the plaintiff's educational experience was substantially interfered with due to the alleged cyberbullying. Strict proof is hereby demanded at time of trial.

COUNT I – NEGLIGENCE

9. No answer required.

10. Denied as a conclusion of law. To the extent the allegations contained in Paragraph 10 are not conclusions of law, they are specifically denied and strict proof is hereby demanded at the time of trial.

11. Denied as a conclusion of law. To the extent the allegations contained in Paragraph 11 are not conclusions of law, they are specifically denied and strict proof is hereby demanded at the time of trial.

12. Denied as a conclusion of law. To the extent the allegations contained in Paragraph 12 are not conclusions of law, they are specifically denied and strict proof is hereby demanded at the time of trial.

13. Denied as a conclusion of law. To the extent the allegations contained in Paragraph 13 are not conclusions of law, they are specifically denied and strict proof is hereby demanded at the time of trial.

14. Denied as a conclusion of law. To the extent the allegations contained in Paragraph 14 are not conclusions of law, they are specifically denied and strict proof is hereby demanded at the time of trial.

15. Denied as a conclusion of law. To the extent the allegations contained in Paragraph 15 are not conclusions of law, they are specifically denied and strict proof is hereby demanded at the time of trial.

AFFIRMATIVE DEFENSES

16. The defendant hereby incorporates by reference the averments set forth in Paragraphs 1 through 15 as though fully set forth herein at length.

17. The plaintiff's claims are barred, in whole or in part, by the doctrine of assumption of the risk.

18. To the extent that the plaintiff seeks to present claims under the state of Washingtonia's anti-cyberbullying legislation, those claims are barred as these statutes create no separate cause of action.

19. The conduct described in the plaintiff's complaint does not rise to the level of cyberbullying.

WHEREFORE, Defendant, Washingtonia State University, respectfully requests that this Honorable Court find in its favor and against the plaintiff's complaint, together with costs and reasonable attorney fees as allowed by law.

Respectfully submitted,

DEFENSE ATTORNEYS, LTD.

By: _____ *J. Nucci* _____

Attorney for Defendant

VERIFICATION

I, Dylan Jeffries, am the Dean of Academics for the Washingtonia State University, and as such am an agent of the defendant capable of signing this verification. I hereby state that the facts set forth in the foregoing answer are true, correct, and accurate to the best of my information and belief. I understand that false statements made herein are subject to penalty of law relating unsworn falsifications to authorities.

Dylan Jeffries
_____

Dylan Jeffries, Agent of the Defendant
February 1, YR-2

EXHIBITS

Exhibit 1

Deposition of Riley Evans
December 28, YR-2, 11:00 a.m.

1   Q: Please tell us your name and where you live.
2
3   A: My name is Riley Evans. I currently live with my parents at 200 West Oxfield
4 Lane in Oaksville, Washingtonia, but during the school year I live in the dorms at Washingtonia
5 Community College.
6
7   Q: What year are you in the college?
8
9   A: I am only a sophomore.
10
11   Q: How old are you?
12
13   A: I'm twenty-one years old.
14
15   Q: How long have you attended the Washingtonia Community College?
16
17   A: I enrolled for Spring YR-2 after I withdrew from the Washingtonia State
18 University, so only one semester.
19
20   Q: When did you withdraw from the Washingtonia State University?
21
22   A: I withdrew on November 3, YR-3. Unfortunately, because it wasn't the end of
23 the fall semester, I didn't get any credits from that semester so when I started at Washingtonia
24 Community College, I only had a full year of college that counted towards my credits.
25
26   Q: What was your grade point average at Washingtonia State University when you
27 withdrew?
28
29   A: I am a really good student and had a 4.0 GPA. I'm very proud of that.
30
31   Q: What is your grade point average at the community college?
32
33   A: Grades haven't come out yet, but I'm hoping it'll be the same. A 4.0. I've never
34 gotten anything lower than an A in my entire life!

1   Q: What do you intend to major in and choose as a career?

2

3   A: I'm not a hundred percent sure yet what my career path is going to be, but I am
4   very interested in politics and may eventually become a lobbyist or even work on the Hill
5   in Washington, D.C. So, I'm leaning towards a major of political science, but don't have to
6   decide my major until next semester.

7

8   Q: Why did you withdraw from Washingtonia State University?

9

10   A: It's a long story, but the main reason is because I was being bullied by other
11   students during a seminar course I enrolled in.

12

13   Q: What was the seminar?

14

15   A: It was called Politics and Social Media, taught by Adjunct Professor Jamie
16   Winstone in the Fall YR-3 semester. It was a three-credit class and met every Monday and
17   Wednesday from 10:00 to 11:50 a.m. I'm not much of an early riser, so the time of the class
18   was perfect.

19

20   Q: Why did you enroll in the class?

21

22   A: Well, like I said, I'm interested in potentially becoming involved in politics and
23   I heard it was a great class that looked at the use of social media in campaigns.

24

25   Q: What do you mean by social media?

26

27   A: You know. Twitter, Facebook, LinkedIn, and all the other websites out there
28   that everyone is using nowadays. The class was supposed to help get an insider's view of the
29   importance of the Internet and social media websites in running a campaign.

30

31   Q: When was your first class?

32

33   A: August 23, YR-3. The first month or so of classes were really not a big deal.
34   Just a bunch of lecturing about how to use social media in campaigns. Professor Winstone used
35   those classes to help familiarize us with the uses of those websites and discuss the philosophy of
36   the use of the Internet to further a campaign. It wasn't until October that things got a little dicey.

37

38   Q: What do you mean by that?

39

40   A: After the first month, Professor Winstone broke our class into two sections.
41   There were only a total of twelve people in the class, so we were broken into two groups
42   of six students. One student from each group was chosen to run as president, and the other
43   students had to help build the campaign.

44

45   Q: Who were the students that were chosen to run for president?

1   A: I was one of them, and Morgan Ritchfield was another. We didn't have much
2   say. Professor Winstone just assigned who the candidates would be. I did not volunteer.
3
4   Q: Who's Morgan Ritchfield?
5
6   A: I didn't really know Morgan too well, but I knew Morgan was also a sopho-
7   more at the time.
8
9   Q: Explain the process of what was supposed to happen once the students were
10   assigned their roles.
11
12   A: The two groups were supposed to use Facebook to create an Internet campaign.
13   The professor created one main group page on Facebook entitled Politics and Social Media
14   YR-3 Election that was a closed group, meaning only Professor Winstone could control who
15   became members. We all had to "friend" or "like" the page so we could use it for our cam-
16   paign. Winstone was the only administrator of the page. I don't really think Winstone ever
17   cared about who looked at the site or who even posted on it. I didn't understand why Winstone
18   even bothered making it a closed group page. We were only supposed to use Facebook and not
19   the other social networking sites out there like Twitter, LinkedIn, et cetera, even though we
20   learned about those sites.
21
22   Q: Was there an election that took place?
23
24   A: There was supposed to be eventually. The last week of class, the class was sup-
25   posed to elect a president based on the campaign.
26
27   Q: I'm showing you what I've marked as Exhibit 9. Do you recognize this?
28
29   A: Yes, I do.
30
31   Q: What is it?
32
33   A: This is a screenshot of the wall of the Facebook page that I just mentioned,
34   where anyone could register and post something about the campaign.
35
36   Q: Is it a fair and accurate copy of the Facebook page as it appeared on
37   November 3, YR-3?
38
39   A: Yes, it is.
40
41   Q: Excuse my ignorance, but I'm not too familiar with Facebook. Can you please
42   generally describe this page and how it works?
43
44   A: Wow. I thought everyone had a Facebook page nowadays. OK, so basically, as
45   you can see at the top of this page, it's called Politics and Social Media YR-3 Election. That's

1 what Professor Winstone named the page for every semester. What you're looking at specifi-
2 cally is the "wall" page. The wall is where people who are members of the page can write com-
3 ments for other members of the page to see. Once a comment is written on the wall, someone
4 can then add a comment or "like" the comment. You can also tell when the posts were written
5 because there are dates after each post.

7 Q: Can you explain to me what the different posts are?

9 A: Sure. As you can see, there are different profile names that can post different
10 comments.

12 Q: Do you know who all the profile names are?

14 A: Not exactly. I know some of them.

16 Q: Which ones do you know?

18 A: RitchfieldYR-3 was Morgan Ritchfield. I was EvansYR-3. As the candidates
19 running for president, Professor Winstone made us use our last name and the year to create our
20 profile name. Other than those two profile names, I could only guess as to who the others were.
21 But, it doesn't take a genius to figure out that names like "Morganmaniac" and "Mritch4prez"
22 were people associated with Ritchfield's campaign.

24 Q: How did this Facebook page affect you?

26 A: This page is eventually what forced me to quit Washingtonia State University.

28 Q: Why do you say that?

30 A: The things that were being written about me were just devastating and untrue.
31 It made a mockery of me, and I just got so embarrassed I had to get out of there.

33 Q: Let's go through that. The first couple posts mention something about cheating
34 in a class. Did you cheat in a class?

36 A: No, that's ridiculous. I'm just a really good student, that's all. That's what made
37 me so mad, because it's not true. And it made me even angrier that the University started an
38 investigation into whether I was cheating.

40 Q: What investigation are you talking about?

42 A: As a result of these stupid posts, I got a summons to appear before the Academic
43 Integrity Board to discuss my grades from the YR-4/YR-3 school year because they suppos-
44 edly had reason to believe that I may have cheated.

1   Q: We'll talk about that investigation more in a moment. For now, let's review
2   some of the posts on Facebook. On October 10, YR-3, Morganmanic wrote something about
3   you making fun of a kid in a wheelchair and telling a racist and crude joke about him. Do you
4   know anything about that?
5
6   A: No, nothing. There is a kid in a wheelchair that was a freshman at Washingtonia
7   State University, but I've never spoken to him or about him. I just thought he was kind of awkward
8   because he kept to himself and never went out. I would never tell a racist joke. That's not my style.
9
10   Q: On October 24, YR-3, RitchfieldYR-3 posted a video claiming it was you. I've
11   marked it as Exhibit 10 and am playing it on the TV screen. Do you recognize this video I've
12   marked as Exhibit 10?
13
14   A: Yes, I do.
15
16   Q: What is it?
17
18   A: It's a video that Morgan Ritchfield posted on Facebook on October 24, YR-3.
19   I saw it on Facebook on October 24, YR-3, and as you can see from the Facebook page, it was
20   posted by the profile "Morgan Ritchfield."
21
22   Q: Is it a fair and accurate copy of the video posted by Ritchfield?
23
24   A: Yes, it is.
25
26   Q: Who's in the video?
27
28   A: That's me and some of my buddies at a party at Gamma Tau Lambda. It wasn't
29   a big deal.
30
31   Q: How old were you then?
32
33   A: It was freshman year, so I was probably nineteen years old.
34
35   Q: What were you drinking?
36
37   A: I'm embarrassed to admit, I was drinking alcohol and doing a keg stand.
38   I certainly don't make a habit of it, but come on. It's college. Doesn't everyone enjoy a beer
39   every now and then in college? I feel like an idiot that someone videotaped it and posted it on the
40   Internet, though. I never would've thought someone would be so mean to do that. And somehow,
41   the university found out about this, too. They were investigating my underage drinking, too.
42
43   Q: I'm showing you what I've marked as Exhibit 8. Do you recognize it?
44
45   A: Yes, I do.

1	Q:	What is it?

2

3   A: This is the summons I received from the Academic Integrity Board to appear
4 on November 16, YR-3, for a hearing regarding my grades and whether I was drinking as
5 a minor.

6

7   Q: Is it a fair and accurate copy of the summons you received?

8

9   A: Yes, it is.

10

11   Q: What ever happened with the investigation?

12

13   A: Nothing. I withdrew before the investigation could proceed.

14

15   Q: Do you know how the school found out about your underage drinking?

16

17   A: I don't know of any other source other than Facebook and this video.

18

19   Q: Do you know who Goldiephd is?

20

21   A: I assume Goldiephd is the graduate student at Washingtonia College of Law
22 that helped me with some of my essays. Her name was Goldie, but I can't remember her last
23 name. She never actually wrote my papers, so this post is a complete lie, but she did help me.
24 Goldie's post made me believe that students other than those in the class were actually viewing
25 the site. The class had gotten quite popular in the last three years, and it doesn't surprise me
26 that someone outside of the class would've viewed it.

27

28   Q: How do you know the class had gotten popular?

29

30   A: The evaluations from the previous classes were available for students to view
31 in order to make an informed decision about whether to take the class.

32

33   Q: Where were the evaluations located?

34

35   A: You could access them in the library or online through the university website.

36

37   Q: How many years had this class been offered?

38

39   A: It was offered every semester from Fall YR-6 through Fall YR-3.

40

41   Q: Did you ever view the evaluations?

42

43   A: Yes, I did.

44

45   Q: When did you view them?

1   A: Before I enrolled in the class.

2

3   Q: How did you view them?

4

5   A: Online.

6

7   Q: I'm showing you what I've marked as Exhibit 7. Do you recognize this?

8

9   A: Yes, I do.

10

11   Q: What is it?

12

13   A: This is a summary of Professor Winstone's evaluations from Fall YR-6 through

14   Spring YR-3 that I saw prior to enrolling in that class.

15

16   Q: Is this a fair and accurate copy of the evaluation summary you saw?

17

18   A: Yes, it is.

19

20   Q: What does the top row of the chart show?

21

22   A: It says FA YR-6, SP YR-5, etc. which represents the semesters Fall YR-6,

23   Spring YR-5, etc. Then, underneath that is the number of students that completed the evalua-

24   tions. For example, in Fall YR-6, ten out of twelve students completed the evaluations.

25

26   Q: Besides the university evaluations, were you aware of any other professor eval-

27   uations of Jamie Winstone before enrolling in Winstone's class?

28

29   A: Yes. I'm a little embarrassed to admit it, but I did go to a website that has

30   professor evaluations on it. It's not exactly an official website, but I find that people are more

31   candid on the website than they tend to be in a university evaluation.

32

33   Q: What is the website called?

34

35   A: TeacherMeter.

36

37   Q: I'm showing you a document that has been marked as Exhibit 13 for identifica-

38   tion purposes. Do you recognize it?

39

40   A: Yes, I sure do.

41

42   Q: What is it?

43

44   A: It is a screen shot of the evaluations for Professor Winstone on the website

45   TeacherMeter.

1   Q: Does Exhibit 13 fairly and accurately show what you saw on the website prior
2   to enrolling in Winstone's class?
3
4   A: Yes, it does.
5
6   Q: Just out of curiosity, what is the thermometer next to Winstone's name?
7
8   A: This is part of why the website is a bit embarrassing. When you go onto this
9   website, you evaluate certain things like overall quality, helpfulness, clarity, easiness, and then
10   there's the final category of hotness. It's no secret that Professor Winstone is really good looking.
11
12   Q: Did you ever talk to anyone about your feelings about the Facebook posts?
13
14   A: Well, I spoke to a few people. I sent a text message to Ritchfield's campaign
15   manager Rob, and I spoke with Professor Winstone.
16
17   Q: Let's discuss first your text messages with Rob. Who is Rob?
18
19   A: Rob Thompson. He was Ritchfield's campaign manager. Rob was
20   "Morganmaniac" on the Facebook page.
21
22   Q: How did you text message Rob?
23
24   A: I had his cell phone number that someone gave me.
25
26   Q: What was his phone number?
27
28   A: (555) 321-4890.
29
30   Q: I'm showing you what has been marked as Exhibit 12 for identification. Do you
31   recognize it?
32
33   A: Yes, I do. It's a screenshot from my cell phone showing the text messages
34   between me and Rob Thompson.
35
36   Q: Is Exhibit 12 a fair and accurate copy of the screenshot of your phone?
37
38   A: Yes, it is. I know that because I'm the one that took the screenshot. When I met
39   with my lawyer, she asked whether I talked to anyone about the video that was on Facebook.
40   When I told her that I sent text messages back and forth with Rob Thompson, she asked me to
41   take a screenshot of the messages. So I did, and then I emailed it to myself and to my lawyer.
42
43   Q: When did you take this screenshot?
44
45   A: I can't remember the exact day, but it was probably early January YR-2.

1   Q: When did you send these text messages between you and Rob Thompson?

2

3   A: Again, I don't know the exact time of day, but I sent them almost imme-
4   diately after Morgan Ritchfield posted the video of me doing the keg stand. That was on
5   October 24, YR-3.

6

7   Q: How did you take the screenshot of the messages? I mean, how can we know
8   that these weren't altered or edited in any way?

9

10   A: Are you questioning my integrity? Of course I didn't alter or edit them. Don't
11   you know how to take a screenshot using an iPhone? Everyone knows how to do that. You just
12   press the home and sleep buttons at the same time and it takes a picture.

13

14   Q: Did you report the Facebook posts to anyone at the university?

15

16   A: I was so frustrated and embarrassed about it that I felt as though I was con-
17   stantly being ridiculed and insulted, so I went to talk to Professor Winstone.

18

19   Q: Do you know whether the university has a policy against bullying?

20

21   A: Yes, there is one.

22

23   Q: How do you know that?

24

25   A: It was in the university handbook that we all get at the beginning of the year.

26

27   Q: I'm showing you a copy of a page from the university handbook marked as
28   Exhibit 5. Do you recognize it?

29

30   A: Yes, that's the portion that discusses cyberbullying and bullying in the university.
31   I got a copy of this particular version the first day of class on August 16, YR-3, via email.

32

33   Q: When did you talk to Professor Winstone about the Facebook posts?

34

35   A: I talked to Professor Winstone on two different occasions. The first time was
36   after class on October 11, and the second time was after class on October 26.

37

38   Q: Let's talk about that first time. What did you tell your professor?

39

40   A: I showed Professor Winstone the Facebook page and pointed out all of the
41   posts about me cheating in class. I explained how that really offended me, and Professor
42   Winstone just kind of shrugged and said something like the posts were nothing more than
43   hard-nosed campaigning and told me not to be so sensitive. When Winstone didn't do any-
44   thing, I thought I could just take the matter into my own hands, and I posted on the site calling
45   Ritchfield a coward.

1   Q: What happened the second time you met with Professor Winstone?

3   A: Again, nothing really happened. I showed Professor Winstone the website again and expressed my anger and embarrassment about the keg stand video. I asked Winstone to take it down since Winstone was the only administrator of the site, but Winstone refused. I also told Professor Winstone how I couldn't concentrate in class, that I had dropped out of student government because I was so embarrassed, and that I was considering leaving the university altogether. Professor Winstone just told me, "Welcome to real life," and that I should consider myself lucky for getting this experience in the safety of university instead of being exposed to it in professional life. Then, the post from goldiephd just put me over the edge. I was so fed up and embarrassed that I decided to leave Washingtonia State University.

13   Q: Did anyone mention these posts to you in person?

15   A: Yes, it was terrible. I had several professors mention them to me and question me about them, not to mention some of the students who ridiculed me on campus saying things like "cheater" and "boozer." It was totally embarrassing.

19   Q: Why aren't you suing Morgan Ritchfield for any of the comments Ritchfield made on the website?

22   A: I don't know. I guess because Morgan's just a student and doesn't have any money. Besides, my lawyer told me to go after the school.

25   Q: Is there anything else you would like to add?

27   A: No, that's all.

I have reviewed this deposition and certify it is an accurate reflection of my statements.

Signed: *Riley Evans*   Date: December 28, YR-2
          Riley Evans

Witnessed: *Steven F. Fairlie*   Date: December 28, YR-2
          Steven F. Fairlie

Exhibit 2

Deposition of Jamie Winstone
December 29, YR-2, 10:00 a.m.

1 Q: Please tell us your name and where you live.
2
3 A: My name is Jamie Winstone. I currently reside at 72 West Dupont Circle,
4 Washingtonia City.
5
6 Q: How old are you?
7
8 A: I'm fifty-two years old.
9
10 Q: Are you married?
11
12 A: You betcha. I've been married for the past twenty years. We have two great
13 kids, an eighteen-year-old son and a sixteen-year-old daughter. My oldest is off to college next
14 year to study physics. I couldn't be more proud of them.
15
16 Q: Are you employed?
17
18 A: Yes, I am. I own my own lobbying firm. I also used to work as an adjunct pro-
19 fessor at the Washingtonia State University, but the university didn't renew my contract for the
20 Spring YR-2 semester so I'm no longer working as an adjunct professor.
21
22 Q: When were you teaching there?
23
24 A: I had a four-year contract with Washingtonia State from Fall YR-6 through
25 Fall YR-3.
26
27 Q: What were you teaching?
28
29 A: I taught a really interesting and relevant course called Politics in Social Media.
30 As a lobbyist, I am all too familiar with how social media is impacting the political scene and
31 how campaigns are using social media with more frequency to relay their messages and garner
32 votes. So, I came up with an idea of holding a small seminar where the students run a simu-
33 lated election and integrate the use of social media. The first month of the class, I taught the
34 class how to use some of the websites like Twitter, Facebook, LinkedIn, et cetera, and showed
35 examples of their use in prior elections and campaigns, like in the Obama/McCain election.

1 Q: How many students were in your classes?

2

3 A: I wanted to keep it small, so I limited my enrollment to twelve students per
4 semester. What we did each semester was hold a mock presidential campaign. So I would
5 assign two students the role of running for president, and the other ten students were split into
6 the two campaign teams. They had to make use of Facebook to run their campaign. Ideally, I
7 would've loved to use Twitter, LinkedIn, and other major social networking sites, but I figured
8 that it would be best to contain the election process solely to one website so I could provide
9 better oversight. So, I created a group on Facebook for each semester. This particular semester
10 it was entitled Politics and Social Media YR-3 Election.

11

12 Q: Who had access to the Facebook page?

13

14 A: Only people who were approved to view the page by me.

15

16 Q: What do you mean by that?

17

18 A: There are a couple different privacy options on Facebook. I created a closed
19 group so that I, as the administrator of the group, would have to approve you to become a
20 member. Once you were approved as a member, you could access the Facebook page, post on
21 it, and see who the other members were.

22

23 Q: How did you decide who could join the Facebook site?

24

25 A: What do you mean? If someone asked to join, I'd say yes.

26

27 Q: Were any students or individuals that were not enrolled in your course approved
28 by you to become members of the site?

29

30 A: Of course. There were seventy some people that were members of the page.
31 Obviously, that includes people who were not students in the class.

32

33 Q: What was your experience with this exercise during other semesters?

34

35 A: From my experience, the students in class really get into it and take the whole
36 thing seriously. So, in the past semesters, there was some typical political mudslinging going
37 back and forth.

38

39 Q: What do you do when you see what you call "typical political mudslinging?"

40

41 A: There's nothing for me to do. It's a campaign election. Of course, there are
42 going to be some feelings hurt.

43

44 Q: What type of boundaries did you provide that your students must follow during
45 the campaign?

1   A: I didn't. The way I saw it, these students were all over eighteen years old. If
2 they can't figure out appropriate boundaries, then they needed to learn a lesson. Besides, in the
3 real political world, there aren't many boundaries. It definitely takes thick skin to play in the
4 political arena.
5
6   Q: Have you ever seen your student evaluations?
7
8   A: Yes, of course. It was important to me what my students thought of me.
9 Fortunately, most of the evaluations were stellar. Seemed to me like I was connecting with my
10 students really well.
11
12   Q: I'm showing you what I've marked as Exhibit 7. Do you recognize this?
13
14   A: Yes, I do. It's the student evaluation summary form from Fall YR-6 through
15 Summer YR-3.
16
17   Q: Did you read these evaluations completely?
18
19   A: Yes, I read every word.
20
21   Q: Did you change any of your class assignments or how the class was run based
22 on any of these evaluations?
23
24   A: Nope. I didn't change a thing.
25
26   Q: Are you aware of any other student evaluations?
27
28   A: I don't know what you mean or what you are talking about.
29
30   Q: I am showing you a document marked Exhibit 13 for identification. Do you
31 recognize it?
32
33   A: Not at all. I've never seen this before. What is it?
34
35   Q: It's a screenshot from a website called TeacherMeter. It is your evaluations
36 by various students. Were you aware that this website existed and that students were making
37 comments about you on this website?
38
39   A: Obviously I wasn't aware. I've never seen this document before. But I'm
40 flattered that I've received a thermometer for hotness. You have to love the minds of our future.
41
42   Q: When was the Politics in Social Media class in the Fall YR-3?
43
44   A: It met on Mondays and Wednesdays from 10:00 to 11:50 a.m. It was a
45 three-credit class.

1   Q: Who was assigned to be the presidential candidates?
2

3   A: Two sophomores, Riley Evans and Morgan Ritchfield. They both seemed to express
4 interest in potentially going into the political arena, and they both volunteered for the position.
5

6   Q: Did you assign the students their profile names for Facebook?
7

8   A: Not all of them. I made sure the two presidential candidates used their last
9 name plus the school year, for example, RitchfieldYR-3, but for the other students, I just left it
10 up to them. I figured it was part of their creativity for purposes of campaigning and didn't want
11 to stifle any good ideas.
12

13   Q: I'm showing you a copy of Exhibit 9. Is this a printout of the wall of the
14 Facebook page from the Fall YR-3 class?
15

16   A: Yes, it is.
17

18   Q: Did you look at this page throughout the semester?
19

20   A: Yes, I typically looked at the page thirty minutes before every class so I could
21 be up to date about what's going on.
22

23   Q: Are you aware of a cyberbullying policy at the University?
24

25   A: Yes. Every year, we got some silly handbook that contained a section about bullying.
26

27   Q: I'm showing you Exhibit 5. Do you recognize this?
28

29   A: Yes, I do. That's the cyberbullying policy of Washingtonia State University that
30 was sent to me via email in the beginning of the semester in August YR-3. We would receive
31 a copy of the policy every academic year. But when I first started, I had to undergo an hour of
32 training on the policy during new hire orientation.
33

34   Q: I'm now showing you Exhibit 11. Do you recognize Exhibit 11?
35

36   A: I do. That is the email that Dean Jeffries sent out at the beginning of the school
37 year, YR-3.
38

39   Q: Is it a fair and accurate copy of the email?
40

41   A: Yes, it is. It is from Dean Jeffries's email address, which is djeffries@
42 washingtonia.nita, and sent to the faculty listserv email address, which is fac/staff_listserv@
43 washingtonia.nita.
44

45   Q: Did you read the email?

1   A: It's the same policy as always, so I probably didn't bother. But I did respond to
2   the email, as I was required to do. That's what the second page of Exhibit 11 is, my response
3   that I received it.

5   Q: The first page of Exhibit 11, which is the email from Dean Jeffries, indicates
6   that there is an attachment. Did you ever open the attachment, and do you know what the
7   attachment was?

9   A: Like I said, I honestly cannot say for sure whether I opened it. I had received
10 the same email every year, so I just assumed that it was the same and didn't bother reading
11 it. But I assume that it was an attachment of the school's policy, which you just showed me
12 marked as Exhibit 5.

14   Q: Did any students complain to you about the Facebook page during the Fall
15 YR-3 semester?

17   A: Yes. Riley Evans came to me twice. First, Riley met with me after class
18 on October 11, YR-3, and our second meeting took place after class on October 26, YR-3. At
19 both meetings, Riley showed me the Facebook page as if I hadn't been paying attention to it.
20 Riley was complaining that the posts were too harsh and untrue or something like that. I basi-
21 cally told Riley to get thicker skin. I mean, Riley wanted to eventually get into politics, and
22 how is that possible if you're going to get this upset over a class project?

24   Q: Did Riley explain to you that Riley was going to drop out of school and had
25 dropped out of extracurricular activities?

27   A: Nope. Not at all. Riley just kept complaining that the other students were being
28 so mean and unfair. Again, I explained that it's better to learn these lessons in the shelter of a
29 university atmosphere as opposed to the real world.

31   Q: Did you ever ask the other students to stop posting mean comments?

33   A: No. It's a free world, and the last thing I want to do is decrease the effectiveness
34 of this exercise by trying to control what people post.

36   Q: Did you ever do anything as a result of the meetings with Riley Evans?

38   A: I wrote an interoffice memo to Dylan Jeffries after my second meeting with
39 Riley, but I didn't do anything after the first meeting.

41   Q: Who's Dylan Jeffries?

43   A: Dylan Jeffries is the Dean of Academics for Washingtonia State University.
44 I was supposed to let Dean Jeffries know of any situations that arose in classes that related to
45 cyberbullying claims, so I was following what I was supposed to be doing.

1   Q: I'm showing you Exhibit 6. Do you recognize it?

2

3   A: Yes, I do.

4

5   Q: What is it?

6

7   A: This is the memo I hand-delivered to Dean Jeffries on October 27, YR-3.

8

9   Q: Is it a fair and accurate copy of the memo you wrote to Dean Jeffries?

10

11   A: Yes, it is.

12

13   Q: Why did you think what Riley Evans told you "wasn't a big deal" and "didn't
14   need to be addressed"?

15

16   A: Like I already told you, I didn't think that any of the comments or posts on
17   Facebook were that big of a deal.

18

19   Q: To the best of your knowledge, did the Washingtonia State University do any
20   investigation into the matter?

21

22   A: I have no idea. But I do know that they did not renew my contract.

23

24   Q: When did your contract expire?

25

26   A: At the end of the Spring YR-3 semester. I was under the impression that I
27   would be teaching the same class in the spring, as it was on the university course roster and
28   being advertised on its academic courses website, but I had a meeting with Dean Jeffries
29   before the end of the fall semester and was told that I would no longer be teaching. Apparently,
30   from what Dean Jeffries told me, the school wasn't too happy with how I handled the Riley
31   situation. Jeffries told me directly that I was being let go because the school had been sued and
32   that I should've been editing and censoring the students more to avoid this type of situation.
33   The university was sued sometime in December. It's not my fault.

34

35   Q: How much were you being paid to teach?

36

37   A: I got $3,000 a credit. With my eighteen-year-old son going into college next
38   year, it sure would've been nice to have that extra money, but things happen.

39

40   Q: Are you here today out of your own accord?

41

42   A: I'd really rather not be involved at all. I got a subpoena from the plaintiff's
43   attorney. I honestly think Riley Evans is just an example of how young students nowadays
44   have a sense of entitlement and need to grow up and get tough. I mean, that's what college is
45   about, right? Preparing students for the real world.

1   Q: Would you like to say anything else?

2

3   A: No.

I have reviewed this deposition and certify it is an accurate reflection of my statements.

Signed: *Jamie Winstone*   Date: December 29, YR-2
            Jamie Winstone

Witnessed: *Steven F. Fairlie*   Date: December 29, YR-2
            Steven F. Fairlie

Exhibit 3

Deposition of Dean Dylan Jeffries
January 4, YR-1, 3:45 p.m.

1   Q: Please tell us your name and where you live.
2
3   A: My name is Dylan Jeffries. I live at 52993 Breeze Point Road, Rightsville,
4   Washingtonia.
5
6   Q: What is your educational and employment background?
7
8   A: I received a bachelor of arts in education in YR-34 from Westmont University.
9   I started working as a high school English teacher in Middlebury, Washingtonia, right after
10   I graduated. I earned my master of arts in higher education in YR-29 and moved on to teach-
11   ing English at Washingtonia Community College. In YR-25, I became a full-time professor
12   of English, specializing in American dialects, at Washingtonia State University. I became ten-
13   ured in YR-21, which is pretty quick for a professor. However, I was routinely evaluated by
14   students as the best professor on campus, I received three teaching awards in four years, and
15   I had published six articles and one *New York Times* bestseller novel. I earned my doctorate in
16   education in YR-15.
17
18   Q: What do you currently do for a living?
19
20   A: I am the Dean of Academics for Washingtonia State University. I was promoted
21   to this position in YR-14.
22
23   Q: What are your duties as the Dean of Academics?
24
25   A: I oversee all of the curriculum and professors at the school. It's a pretty big
26   university with about 35,000 students. There are hundreds of classes offered each semester.
27   My goal is to ensure all the courses being taught meet the rigorous academic standards for
28   which this university is known. I interview, hire, evaluate, and mentor the professors. I am
29   also the head of the Academic Integrity Board, which investigates and disciplines students
30   for violations of the academic honor code, such as cheating. A subsidiary of that board is the
31   Disciplinary Board, which looks into allegations that students violated any other school policy.
32   I'm also the head of that board.
33
34   Q: To your knowledge, does the university have any policies on bullying?
35
36   A: Yes, the school has an anti-bullying policy, as well as one against cyberbully-
37   ing. I helped develop it after the state legislature passed the School Cyberbullying Act of YR-6.

1   Q: Please describe the cyberbullying policy.
2

3   A: The policy prohibits students from using any sort of school technology to harass
4 or intimidate anyone connected with the university. It includes using school computers to post
5 to outside websites and using outside computers to post to school websites.
6

7   Q: Why was this policy developed?
8

9   A: The policy was developed to be in compliance with the state anti-cyberbullying
10 statute.
11

12   Q: You are being shown a document that is labeled Exhibit 5. Do you recognize
13 this?
14

15   A: Yes, it is a copy of the university's cyberbullying policy.
16

17   Q: Is it a fair and accurate copy of the policy?
18

19   A: Yes.
20

21   Q: Do you have any involvement with the University's anti-bullying policies?
22

23   A: Yes.
24

25   Q: Please describe your involvement.
26

27   A: I am responsible for ensuring every professor and student completes the man-
28 datory annual training on the cyberbullying policy. I also respond to any complaints or con-
29 cerns professors bring to me in accordance with the policy.
30

31   Q: How is training for the faculty conducted?
32

33   A: When the policy was implemented, we held several training sessions to ensure
34 all existing faculty and staff were trained on the policy in person. Each new faculty member
35 receives an hour of training on the policy during their new hire orientation. After that, they are
36 emailed a copy of the policy at the start of each academic year. They are required to reply by
37 email certifying that they have reviewed the policy within one week of receiving the reminder.
38

39   Q: Why do you not conduct a live annual training on this policy?
40

41   A: We tried the first year, but it just wasn't feasible to have a time that fit the sched-
42 ules of all of the professors and staff. Including the part-time, full-time, and adjunct profes-
43 sors, we have over 200 professors. The professors are especially hard to schedule because they
44 travel during semester breaks or are on sabbatical. The administration decided that all of our

1   employees were professional and could be trusted to complete the training on their own after
2   the initial live session. We have not had any problems with this method.
3
4   Q: How are students trained on the cyberbullying policy?
5
6   A: Like the faculty and staff, each student receives training on the policy when
7   they enter the university. Each student receives an email at the beginning of each fall semester
8   reminding them of the policy.
9
10   Q: I'm showing you what has been marked as Exhibit 11 for identification. Do you
11   recognize it?
12
13   A: Yes, I do. This is the email that I sent to the faculty and staff listserv on
14   August 15, YR-3.
15
16   Q: It indicates there is an attachment to the email. What is the attachment?
17
18   A: That is a copy of the YR-3 Cyber Bullying Policy, which you just showed me
19   as Exhibit 5.
20
21   Q: Whose e-mail is djeffries@washingtonia.nita?
22
23   A: That's my email address.
24
25   Q: Who did this email go out to?
26
27   A: I have an email listserv that includes all faculty members and staff members.
28   They all received a copy of this through the email address fac/staff_listserv@washingtonia.nita.
29
30   Q: Did you ever receive a response from Jamie Winstone indicating that Winstone
31   received the email?
32
33   A: Yes, I did receive a response from Winstone three days later on August 18.
34   That's the second page of Exhibit 11.
35
36   Q: What is the process for evaluating a complaint of cyberbullying?
37
38   A: First, the professor has to become aware of the situation, either through a stu-
39   dent report or by personal observation. Once that happens, the professor must inform us of
40   the situation, including the students involved and the circumstances surrounding the alleged
41   bullying. After we receive the professor's report, the Disciplinary Board decides on a case-by-
42   case basis how to handle the issue. Some cases we can dismiss right away. Others require more
43   investigation. The reporting professor plays a key role in the investigation because he or she
44   has the first-hand knowledge of what happened.

1   Q: Do you know a person named Jamie Winstone?

2

3   A: Yes, Jamie Winstone used to be a professor at this university and taught a social
4 media class in the political science department, as well as introductory civics classes.

5

6   Q: What do you mean by "used to be a professor?"

7

8   A: Winstone was an adjunct professor who taught on a four year contract with the
9 school. Jamie was hired in August YR-6, and the contract was terminated after the Fall YR-3
10 semester.

11

12   Q: Why was Winstone's contract terminated?

13

14   A: Well, Winstone was a very well-liked professor whose classes always filled up.
15 The annual evaluations were satisfactory. I never told Winstone the reason for being fired was
16 because we were sued by Evans. I would never say such a thing. The one big negative against
17 Winstone, though, was the rise in complaints on the students' class evaluations.

18

19   Q: What sort of complaints did students make?

20

21   A: They were mostly along the lines of the professor not controlling the class
22 discussion and atmosphere. We strive to make this school a positive learning environment, so
23 complaints of this type are taken very seriously.

24

25   Q: When did you first start receiving these complaints?

26

27   A: Fall YR-4.

28

29   Q: I'm showing you Exhibit 7. Do you recognize that?

30

31   A: Yes, I do.

32

33   Q: What is it?

34

35   A: This is the Professor Evaluation Summary for Jamie Winstone for the politics
36 and social media class.

37

38   Q: Is it the regular practice of the university to make this type of document?

39

40   A: Yes, it is.

41

42   Q: Is Exhibit 7 kept in the regular course of a regularly conducted activity at the
43 university?

44

45   A: Yes, it is.

1   Q: How is the exhibit created?

2

3   A: My office collects the evaluations of professors and adjunct professors each
4 semester. We compile all of the information for the same professor and create this document
5 so it's easier for students to look at a professor's evaluations for all of his or her semesters.

6

7   Q: Did you ever discuss the evaluations with Winstone?

8

9   A: Each professor is given the results of the student evaluations, so I am sure Winstone
10 was aware that it was an issue, but I never had a direct conversation with Winstone about it.

11

12   Q: How are professors evaluated?

13

14   A: Each professor has a set of goals for the academic year, such as course enroll-
15 ment, participation in meetings and boards within the school, and other professional metrics.
16 Additionally, students complete a standard evaluation of the professors at the end of each semester.
17 These student evaluations are compiled and made available on the university website. We examine
18 them for trends in how students perceive the professors. We want to ensure students are getting a
19 good education from quality professors, so a downward trend in an area is reason for concern.

20

21   Q: Besides the university evaluations, are you aware of any other evaluations of
22 Winstone?

23

24   A;   I don't know what you are talking about.

25

26   Q: I'm showing you what I've marked as Exhibit 13 for identification. Do you
27 recognize this?

28

29   A: No, I don't. I've never seen this before.

30

31   Q: You are being shown a document marked as Exhibit 6. Do you recognize this?

32

33   A: Yes, it is a memo Winstone sent to my office in October YR-3. It describes a meet-
34 ing with one of the students in the Politics and Social Media seminar taught by Winstone each
35 semester. It was a very popular class. Apparently a student, Riley Evans, who brought this lawsuit
36 against the University, was complaining about the behavior of another student in the class.

37

38   Q: What action did you take as a result of this memo?

39

40   A: None.

41

42   Q: Why not?

43

44   A: Well, as you can see in the memo, there doesn't appear to be much more
45 than hurt feelings. We rely on professors as the frontline investigators when it comes

1   to complaints like this. Since Winstone did not think it was serious, we followed that
2   recommendation.
3
4   Q: Do you know Riley Evans?
5
6   A: You mean besides from this lawsuit claiming cyberbullying?
7
8   Q: Yes, did you know Riley Evans before this lawsuit?
9
10   A: Yes. Unfortunately, Evans's name came up before the academic integrity and
11   the disciplinary boards shortly before Winstone sent me this memo.
12
13   Q: Why were the boards investigating Riley Evans?
14
15   A: The disciplinary board was investigating a report of underage drinking and a
16   report that Riley Evans paid a graduate student to write essays for Evan's freshman year.
17
18   Q: How were these reports made?
19
20   A: We have a way of emailing the disciplinary board anonymously on our website.
21   We find that fosters students to make reports. If they have to identify themselves when making
22   the reports, then oftentimes they will not do so out of fear of the reported student finding out.
23   The disciplinary board received a video via email from an anonymous student that showed
24   Evans drinking at an underage party. We also received an anonymous email regarding Evans's
25   cheating. Someone sent a copy of a Facebook post from "Goldiephd."
26
27   Q: I'm showing you a copy of what I've marked as Exhibit 14. Do you recognize it?
28
29   A: Yes, I do. This is a fair and accurate copy of the email that I received anony-
30   mously on October 31, YR-3, at 2:10 p.m. It has attached to it the video of Evans doing a keg
31   stand and the screenshot of a post by Goldiephd on Facebook.
32
33   Q: What did you do as a result of receiving this email?
34
35   A: Normally, the board invites the student to speak with us about the allegations
36   of underage drinking and cheating, so we sent a summons requiring Evans to show up for a
37   hearing where we would discuss the allegations.
38
39   Q: Do you recognize this document, which is marked as Exhibit 8?
40
41   A: Yes, it is the summons the disciplinary board sent to Evans regarding the hear-
42   ing we required Evans to attend.
43
44   Q: Is it a fair and accurate copy of that summons?

1   A: Yes.

2

3   Q: What was the result of the investigation into Riley Evans's grades?

4

5   A: The board never completed its investigation because Evans withdrew from the

6 university shortly after Winstone sent my office that memo.

7

8   Q: Did you or anyone else from the disciplinary or academic integrity boards view

9 the entire Facebook page from Winstone's class?

10

11   A: No, I didn't see how that was necessary.

12

13   Q: Is there anything else you'd like to add?

14

15   A: No, there isn't.

I have reviewed this deposition and certify it is an accurate reflection of my statements.

Signed: *Dylan Jeffries*   Date: January 4, YR-1
             Dylan Jeffries

Witnessed: *Steven F. Fairlie*   Date: January 4, YR-1
              Steven F. Fairlie

Exhibit 4

Deposition of Morgan Ritchfield
January 5, YR-1, 11:00 a.m.

1 Q: Please tell us your name and where you live.

2

3 A: My name is Morgan Ritchfield. I live in Room 5B, Naylor Hall, on the campus

4 of Washingtonia State University, Rightsville, Washingtonia.

5

6 Q: How old are you?

7

8 A: I'm twenty-one years old.

9

10 Q: Where are you from?

11

12 A: I was born and raised right here in Rightsville.

13

14 Q: What do you do for a living?

15

16 A: I am currently a senior at Washingtonia State University. I'm majoring in eco-

17 nomics. I started out in philosophy, but my parents convinced me to get a degree that I can use

18 as soon as I graduate. It's been a dream of mine since I was a kid to go to school here. This has

19 been the best experience of my life.

20

21 Q: How long have you been enrolled at the university?

22

23 A: Since Fall YR-4. I've been here for my entire school career.

24

25 Q: How are your grades?

26

27 A: Well, I started out pretty rough because I was partying too much, but I've man-

28 aged to bring them up to a 2.97 GPA. Hopefully, I can get above a 3.0 by the time I graduate.

29

30 Q: What do you plan to do when you graduate?

31

32 A: I want to work for an economics think tank in D.C., someplace I can apply

33 economic theory to politics. I haven't really been interested in politics, but some of the classes

34 I've taken here at WSU have really piqued my interest.

1   Q: Do you remember what classes you took in the Fall YR-3?
2
3   A: Of course. I took macroeconomics, introductory German, calculus, modern
4   American poetry, and politics and social media.
5
6   Q: What was the politics and social media class?
7
8   A: It was a three-credit class that met on Monday and Wednesday mornings from
9   10:00 to 11:50. That was the main class that got me interested in politics. It explored how
10 modern politics are influenced by all forms of social media—blogs, Twitter, social networks,
11 webpages, et cetera. It was really awesome.
12
13 Q: Who taught the course?
14
15 A: Professor Jamie Winstone, who is amazing. Professor Winstone really gave us
16 an in-depth, hands-on experience of how campaigns really work and how social media has
17 transformed the campaign landscape.
18
19 Q: Why did you decide to take the class?
20
21 A: I wanted to take a political science course, and this one had great reviews. I
22 looked at the student evaluations and Professor Winstone was rated very highly on how interest-
23 ing the class was, how much experience the professor had, and for having a relaxed atmosphere
24 in class. It sounded like the perfect interesting, laid-back class to balance out my other classes.
25
26 Q: You are being shown a document marked Exhibit 7. Do you recognize it?
27
28 A: Yes, it's the summary of student evaluations for Professor Winstone that I
29 looked at when I was deciding whether to take the politics and social media class. All the stu-
30 dents can access it on the school's website.
31
32 Q: Is it a fair and accurate copy of the evaluations you examined?
33
34 A: Yes.
35
36 Q: I'm now showing you Exhibit 13. Do you recognize it?
37
38 A: Yes, I do. It looks to be a screen shot of Professor Winstone's evaluation on a
39 website called TeacherMeter.
40
41 Q: Did you look at this website before enrolling in the class?
42
43 A: Yes, I did. Most students nowadays go to this website to get the real inside
44 scoop on a professor. Exhibit 13 is a fair and accurate copy of how the website looked as of
45 August YR-3.

1   Q: What type of work did you do in the class?

2

3   A: There were a lot of little side assignments, but the major project was a semester-
4 long "presidential election" campaign. The class was divided in half, with Professor Winstone
5 picking a student to be the candidate, and the rest of the students were campaign staff.

6

7   Q: How many students were in the class?

8

9   A: Twelve, although one dropped out halfway through the semester.

10

11   Q: Who were the presidential candidates in your class?

12

13   A: I was one, and Riley Evans was my opponent.

14

15   Q: Who won the election?

16

17   A: I did, by default, since Evans dropped out of school during that semester.

18

19   Q: What type of social media was involved in the campaign?

20

21   A: Mostly Facebook. Although we learned about the use of other social media
22 tools, Professor Winstone only let us post on Facebook, so Winstone created a group called
23 Politics and Social Media YR-3 Election. We used it to introduce the candidates and their plat-
24 forms, plus publish news or updates. Anyone could post comments about the candidates, the
25 campaign, et cetera.

26

27   Q: When you say "anyone" could post comments, what do you mean by that?

28

29   A: Anyone that was a member of the group could post comments.

30

31   Q: How did someone become a member of the Facebook group?

32

33   A: That's easy. As long as you had a Facebook profile page, you could ask to join
34 the group. Professor Winstone was the administrator, so Winstone determined whether you
35 could become a member or not.

36

37   Q: You are being shown a document labeled Exhibit 9. Do you recognize this?

38

39   A: Yes.

40

41   Q: What is it?

42

43   A: It's a printout of the Facebook page that was used in the class, for the campaign.
44 This printout of the page shows the Facebook page as of November 3, YR-3.

1   Q: Is it a fair and accurate copy of the Facebook page?

2

3   A: Yes, as far as I can tell. It looks like all of the posts that I remember.

4

5   Q: Do you recognize any of the screen names on this printout?

6

7   A: Yes, I recognize most of them. "RitchfieldYR-3" is me, "Morganmaniac" was

8   my campaign manager, Rob Thompson, "Mritch4prez" was Misty Wellman, my spokeswoman,

9   and "EvansYR-3" was Riley Evans. I think "Evanslvr" was someone on Evans's campaign

10   staff. I don't know who "Goldiephd" was, but anyone could post on the site, like I said.

11

12   Q: How do you know who had these screen names?

13

14   A: Both candidates were required to use our last names and the year as our screen

15   names, that way everyone would know it was us who was posting the messages. I know Rob

16   and Misty's screen names because we chose them at our first campaign meeting. I assume

17   Evans did the same thing for the staff on that campaign.

18

19   Q: Why did you make the first comment about integrity?

20

21   A: I kind of took a page from the other campaigns I've watched over the last year,

22   for state or federal offices. One big part of getting people to vote for you is showing that you

23   have integrity and the other guy doesn't. I wanted to be first out of the box to use that tactic

24   and stake the claim on that concept.

25

26   Q: Did you know anything specific about Riley Evans that made you believe Evans

27   did not have integrity?

28

29   A: Not me, personally, but some stuff came up during our campaign meetings.

30   Other people knew Evans from previous classes. I told them they could post anything they

31   wanted, as long as they had proof to back it up.

32

33   Q: Let's discuss the post by the profile name Morgan Ritchfield that has a video

34   attached to it. What is the content of that post?

35

36   A: I uploaded a link to a video I had of Evans getting drunk and doing a keg stand

37   at a fraternity party during freshman year. I think it was February or March YR-4. I had to

38   use my own personal Facebook profile name, Morgan Ritchfield, because for some reason

39   Facebook wouldn't let me upload the video by using my RitchfieldYR-3 page.

40

41   Q: Where did you get the video?

42

43   A: I took it myself with my iPhone. I was at the party and saw Evans chugging beer,

44   doing shots, and generally acting like an idiot. I didn't know who Evans was then, but I thought

45   it was funny and started recording it on my phone. I forgot about it until I was going through

     my phone during class one day in Fall YR-3 and recognized Evans as the person in the video.

46

1   Q: Why did you upload the video?

2

3   A: Evans was going on and on in class about being an upstanding citizen who
4   always follows the rules. This was direct proof against that, so I figured it had to be posted. The
5   people have a right to know when candidates are lying to them. Plus, outside of class, I totally
6   heard Evans brag about being able to do the longest keg stand ever. What a joke. That's more
7   like the shortest keg stand ever.

8

9   Q: You are watching a video that is labeled Exhibit 10. Do you recognize this?

10

11   A: Yes, that's the video I made of Evans at the party and linked to Facebook.

12

13   Q: Is this a fair and accurate copy of that video?

14

15   A: Yes, that's the whole video I shot.

16

17   Q: Did Riley Evans ever speak to you about the things that were posted on the
18   Facebook page?

19

20   A: No, Evans never came to me, but I do know that Evans sent text messages to
21   my campaign manager, Rob Thompson.

22

23   Q: I'm showing you Exhibit 12. Are these the text messages to which you
24   just referred?

25

26   A: Yes, I believe they are.

27

28   Q: How did you know that Evans sent text messages to Rob Thompson?

29

30   A: Because Thompson forwarded them to me and we talked about them.

31

32   Q: I'm confused. What exactly does Exhibit 12 show?

33

34   A: That's a screenshot of the text messages between Riley Evans and Rob Thompson.

35

36   Q: OK, but you said that Rob forwarded them to you. So this is a screenshot from
37   your phone? Or from Rob's phone?

38

39   A: Oh, I understand your confusion. It's actually a screenshot from my phone. So
40   Rob had forwarded them from me to my phone.

41

42   Q: So who wrote which color?

43

44   A: Obviously, the green boxes are Riley Evans and the white boxes are
45   Rob Thompson.

1   Q: How can you be so sure?

2

3   A: Rob told me. Plus, the green box says "Riley Evans."

4

5   Q: When did Rob forward these to you?

6

7   A: October 31.

8

9   Q: Do you know when Rob received them?

10

11   A: No.

12

13   Q: Do you know Evans's phone number or Rob's phone number?

14

15   A: Not off the top of my head, no.

16

17   Q: Were you aware that these statements were upsetting Evans?

18

19

20   A: No, not at all. I don't see why they were upsetting either. I mean, even the text

21   message Evans sent to Rob Thompson didn't actually say that Evans was upset. It's not like

22   any of the statements on Facebook were lies. If Evans didn't want people to know about that

23   stuff, Evans shouldn't have done those things in public.

24

25   Q: Did you write, or encourage anyone to write, statements with the intention to

26   bully Riley Evans?

27

28   A: No, not at all. I have nothing against Evans, at all. We barely know each other.

29   This was only part of the class. We were role playing.

30

31   Q: Are you aware that Riley Evans dropped out of school?

32

33   A: Yeah, I heard something about that. I figured it was because of the academic

34   integrity investigation that started after everyone found out about Evans's cheating and under-

35   age drinking.

36

37   Q: Are you aware of the school's policy on cyberbullying?

38

39   A: Yes, I remember reading about the policy in the university handbook I was

40   given during freshmen orientation. We all had to sign a paper acknowledging we read and

41   understood the policy. The university also sends out a copy by email in August of each school

42   year. We have to reply that we received it.

43

44   Q: You are being shown what is marked as Exhibit 5. Do you recognize this?

1   A: Yes, it's a copy of the cyberbullying policy from the university handbook.
2
3   Q: Is this a fair and accurate copy of the policy?
4
5   A: Yes
6
7   Q: Did you ever consider that the comments on the campaign bulletin board were
8   cyberbullying?
9
10   A: No, not at all. Everything that was on that board was true. And it's not like we
11   posted it on the front page of the school newspaper.
12
13   Q: Did Professor Winstone ever speak with you about the Facebook posts or com-
14   ments made during the campaign?
15
16   A: No, never. In fact, I got an A in that course, which really helped bring my GPA up.
17
18   Q: Did anyone from the school administration ever speak to you about the
19   Facebook posts?
20
21   A: No.
22
23   Q: Were you disciplined for the Facebook posts?
24
25   A: No, I've never been in trouble at school.
26
27   Q: Well, that's not exactly true, is it?
28
29   A: What are you talking about?
30
31
32   Q: Didn't you lie on a college application to University of Transylvania about your
33   high school GPA and then get caught by the University of Transylvania?
34
35   A: Well, yeah, but that's a different school. I meant I've never been in trouble at
36   this school. At Washingtonia State University.
37
38   Q: Whatever happened with the issue at the University of Transylvania?
39
40   A: Nothing, really. I got a phone call from the admissions department basically
41   telling me that they got my transcript from high school and the GPAs did not match up. They
42   strongly suggested that I withdraw my application so as to avoid any further issues or penal-
43   ties, and I did. I put the wrong GPA on my application because I really wanted to go to that
44   school and I figured they would never find out.

1   Q: Is there anything else you would like to say?
2
3   A: No.

I have reviewed this deposition and certify it is an accurate reflection of my statements.

Signed: _*Morgan Ritchfield*_   Date: January 5, YR-1
        Morgan Ritchfield

Witnessed: _*Steven F. Fairlie*_   Date: January 5, YR-1
           Steven F. Fairlie

Exhibit 5

Selected Portions of Washingtonia State University
Student Handbook

Section 6640 — Cyberbullying

6640.1 The Washingtonia State University Board strives to provide a safe, positive learning climate for students in the schools. Therefore, it shall be the policy of the university to maintain an educational environment in which cyberbullying in any form is not tolerated.

6640.1a All forms of cyberbullying by university students is hereby prohibited. Anyone who engages in cyberbullying in violation of this policy shall be subject to appropriate discipline.

6640.1b Students who have been the victim of cyberbullying shall promptly report such incidents to any staff member.

6640.1c Complaints of cyberbullying shall be investigated promptly, and corrective action shall be taken when a complaint is verified.

6640.1d The university shall annually inform students that cyberbullying of students will not be tolerated.

6640.1e Each student shall be responsible for respecting the rights of his or her fellow students and to ensure an atmosphere free of all forms of cyberbullying.

6640.2 "Cyberbullying" is the repeated use by one or more students of a verbal, written, or electronic expression, or any combination thereof, directed at the victim that creates a hostile environment for the victim or interferes with the victim's rights at school.

6640.2a "Technology" includes, but is not limited to, telephones, computers, game consoles, and personal electronic devices such as portable music players, computer tablets, cellular telephones, and smartphones.

6640.2b "Electronic communications" include, but are not limited to, any written, oral, or visual imagery sent through technology included in (A) above. Examples of communications include websites, electronic mail, instant messages, and postings to social media or shared media sites, either within the school's domain or in the public domain through use of the school's equipment.

6640.2c A "hostile environment" is a situation which is permeated with intimidation, ridicule, or insult that is sufficiently severe or pervasive to substantially interfere with the victim's educational performance, opportunities, or benefits.

6640.3 A violation of this policy shall subject the offending student to appropriate disciplinary action, consistent with the student discipline code, which may include verbal or written reprimands, suspension, expulsion, or notification to the appropriate authorities.

Exhibit 6

October 27, YR-3, Memo to Dean Dylan Jeffries from Jamie Winstone

TO: Dean Jeffries

FROM: Jamie Winstone, Adjunct Professor, Department of Political Science

DATE: October 27, YR-3

SUBJECT: Student meeting

....

Dean Jeffries:

I met with Riley Evans, a student in my Politics and Social Media class yesterday. Riley expressed concerns about the content of student comments on our Facebook page. As you know, my seminar involves a mock presidential election and part of that process is allowing students to conduct a campaign using social media. As such, I created a Facebook page entitled Politics and Social Media YR-3 Election, on which students can post comments and information about the "candidates" for that semester's elections.

Evans was complaining about comments fellow students had posted about Evans's academic and moral integrity. I review the postings on the bulletin board every day before class. Nothing that was posted comes close to crossing the line. I did my best to encourage Evans to stay with the class, explaining that the purpose of the class was to simulate real-world scenarios. It is natural that some feelings might get hurt, but I believe it is necessary in order to promote a dialogue and really get students to think about the impact words have on society, especially in our instant-news world.

If you have any questions about this, let me know.

J. Winstone

Winstone

Exhibit 7

Washingtonia State University Professor Evaluation Summary

Teaching the Minds of Tomorrow

Professor Evaluation Summary

This displays the average grade of student evaluations received by the professor listed below for the class listed below. Evaluations are completed prior to the end of each semester by all students in the class. Professors are rated on a scale of 1 to 5, with 1 being the lowest ("do not agree at all") and 5 being the highest ("agree completely").

Professor: JAMIE WINSTONE

Class: POLITICS AND SOCIAL MEDIA

Semester/Number of Evaluations	FA YR-6 (10/12)	SP YR-5 (9/12)	FA YR-5 (7/12)	SP YR-4 (9/12)	FA YR-4 (8/12)	SP YR-3 (9/12)
Professor was enthusiastic and knowledgeable	5.0	5.0	5.0	5.0	5.0	5.0
Professor managed class effectively	4.4	5.0	4.4	4.1	4.5	4.3
Professor responded to student questions	4.2	3.0	3.2	1.9	2.3	1.9
Professor responded to student concerns	2.3	1.7	3.2	2.8	2.7	2.5
Professor encouraged differing opinions	4.8	5.0	4.0	3.6	3.5	3.0
Professor maintained respectful learning environment	3.0	3.0	2.9	2.7	2.5	3.0

Student Supplemental Comments

This class rocks! This class was so much fun and so relevant . . .

The idea of this class is great, but Professor Winstone really let some students say whatever they wanted to on the Facebook pages. Some of the comments are harsh!!!

This class will definitely help prepare me for the real world. Social media is the way to go nowadays for everything. If you can get into this class, you definitely should! But don't be dumb and volunteer to be one of the presidential candidates. It can get a little vicious and personal!

Exhibit 8

Washingtonia State University Academic Integrity Board Summons

Teaching the Minds of Tomorrow

SUMMONS

___Academic Integrity Board (Disciplinary Board)___	*
Department	*
	*
IN THE MATTER OF	* Docket No.: YR-3-632
	*
___Riley Evans___	*
Respondent	*

TO:

___Riley Evans___
Name of Respondent

___200 W. Oxford Lane___
Street Address

___Oaksville, Washingtonia 012346___
Name of Respondent

YOU ARE COMMANDED TO:

_x_ Appear and testify in the above-entitled matter at the place, date, and time indicated below for:

Disciplinary Board Hearing as a result of allegations of cheating and underage drinking during the YR-4/YR-3 academic year.

And there to remain until discharged by the Academic Integrity Board by which you are summoned to testify to the truth, to the best of your knowledge.

By order of said Disciplinary Board, this 31st day of   October   , YR-3 , at Washingtonia State University.

Location to appear: Office of the Dean of Academics

Date and time to appear: November 16, YR-3, 9:00 a.m.

Dylan Jeffries
Signature of Officer Issuing Subpoena

Exhibit 9

Facebook Screenshots

 Search for people, places and things   Home Find Friends Name

Politics and Social Media YR-3 Election   [Liked]

Education   Edit Info

Wall   Politics and Social Media....   Everyone (Most Recent)

Share: Status   Photo   Link   Video   Question

Write something......

Wall

   Hidden Posts

Info

Friend Activity

Photos

EDIT

About

This Facebook Page is created for the Politics and Social Media Course taught.....
More

17
like this

3
talking about this

 Morganmaniac
Success!!!! Evans drops out of the campaign...and school! Good riddance to the lying, cheating, racist cry baby. See...social media does work in campaigns!!!
Like   Comment   November 3, YR-3 at 12:08pm

    Mritch4prez Yay! I heard Evans got a summons from the Disciplinary Board and was too chicken to face the facts so quitting school was easier. Loser!!!
   Like   November 3, YR-3 at 12:10pm

   Write a comment...

 EvansYR-3
Who's the rat? Who sent these things to the Disciplinary Board? Speak now or forever hold your peace.
Like   Comment   November 1, YR-3 at 12:36pm

    Morganmaniac What are you worried about Evans? If none of this is true, then why do you care? Cry baby
   Like   November 2, YR-3 at 8:57am

    Mritch4prez @Morganmaniac - I totally agree! Evans is a loser and a punk. Definitely not capable of being president...not even in a college class!!!
   Like   November 2, YR-3 at 8:57am

    EvansYR-3 Why are you guys so mean? This page is meant to help your candidate, not put me down! I can't belive all of this
   Like   November 2, YR-3 at 8:58am

    Morganmaniac waaaaaaa waaaaaa
   Like   November 2, YR-3 at 8:58am

   Write a comment...

Goldiephd

Hey. I am a law student at Washingtonia College of Law (WCL)...just wanted to share my two cents. Evans paid me to write freshman essays last year...I totally believe the cheating stories.

Like   Comment   October 31, YR-3 at 12:04pm

EvansYR-3 did you send this to this disciplinary board? How dare you?

Like   November 1, YR-3 at 12:35pm

Mritch4prez Goldie doesn't need to! Everyone knows you're a cheat and a liar!

Like   November 1, YR-3 at 12:40pm

> Write a comment...

EvansYR-3

Be sure to vote for the candidate who is down to earth, doesn't kiss up to professors, and gets things done!!!!

Like   Comment   October 24, YR-3 at 2:01pm

Morganmaniac you can't possibly think that describes you!! Get real. You're such a loser.

Like   October 24, YR-3 at 2:01pm

> Write a comment...

Morgan Ritchfield

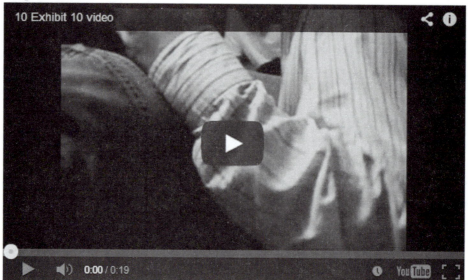

10 Exhibit 10 video

0:00 / 0:19

Like   Comment   October 24, YR-3 at 1:06pm

Morgan Ritchfield Hot off the press!!! Get a load of Evans totally wasted at the Gamma Tau Lambda party!! How old is Evans again? Oh Yeah...19! HAHAHAHAHA

Like   October 24, YR-3 at 1:09pm

EvansYR-3 Morgan...that's a low blow! Where did you get this video? I can't believe you posted this!

Like   October 24, YR-3 at 1:10pm

EvansYR-3 You can't even prove that video is of me. Nice try...you're such a sleezeball, Ritchfield. Why don't you go suck up to the professors some more?

Like   October 24, YR-3 at 1:57pm

Mritch4prez

Boo hoo!!! Cry-Baby Riley ran to the professor. If you can't take the heat, Evans, drop out of the race! Better yet, drop out of school!

Like **Comment** October 13, YR-3 at 11:58am

EvansYR-3

Great job, Ritchfield...sending your goons out to smear my name becuase you're too much of a coward to confront me yourself. Yeah right, you have integrity...

Like **Comment** October 11, YR-3 at 1:48pm

Morganmaniac

News flash...Evans definitely cheated last semester. Some grad student wrote Evans' freshman essays! Don't vote for a condidate who can't even do their own work!!!

Like **Comment** October 10, YR-3 at 12:18pm

Mitch4prez Yep! I was in the same political science class last spring...Evans def copied off a girl's test in the final & when I asked about it, Evans said it was no big deal.

Like October 10, YR-3 at 12:23pm

Morganmaniac What a jerk! Totally belive it though, after I heard Evans making fun of a kid in a wheelchair - told a totally racist & crude joke about him.

Like October 10, YR-3 at 12:27pm

RitchfieldYR-3 See folks...proof that I'm the candidate with integrity in this race!!!

Like October 10, YR-3 at 12:38pm

> Write a comment...

RitchfieldYR-3

Remember folks - vote for the candidate with integrity, not the one who only pretends to care.

Like **Comment** October 6, YR-3 at 11:42pm

Morganmaniac Don't listen to Evans...a liar and a cheat!

Like October 6, YR-3 at 12:04pm

Evanslvr You can't say that w/out proof! Stop trying to be negative. Ritchfield's campaign is a joke.

Like October 6, YR-3 at 12:06pm

> Write a comment...

Jamie Winstone

What an exciting new year! I can't wait to see all of the great ways you utilize Facebook for purposes of this election!

Like **Comment** October 6, YR-3 at 11:26pm

There are no more posts to show.

Exhibit 10

Keg Stand Video
(on CD-ROM)

Exhibit 11

Emails between Dean Dylan Jeffries and Jamie Winstone

From: djeffries@washingtonia.nita
To: fac/staff_listserv@washingtonia.nita
Subject: Washingtonia Cyberbullying Policy
Date: August 15, YR-3

Dear Faculty & Staff,

As you know, Washingtonia University takes cyberbullying very seriously. With this policy, we hope to aid you in preventing and remedying any cyberbullying you become aware of in your capacity as an employee at this university. The University's anti-cyberbullying policy is attached.

You **MUST** respond via email to me that you have reviewed this policy within **SEVEN** days of this email.

Sincerely,

Dean Jeffries
Dean of Students
Washingtonia University
1228 Washingtonia Lane

From: jwinstone@washingtonia.nita
To: djeffries@washingtonia.nita
Subject: Washingtonia Cyberbullying Policy
Date: August 18, YR-3

Dean Jeffries –

I received your email about cyberbullying. I look forward to another exciting semester!

Jamie Winstone, Adjunct Professor
Washingtonia University

Exhibit 12

Text Messages between Riley Evans and Rob Thompson

Exhibit 13

Student Evaluations Screenshot on TeacherMeter

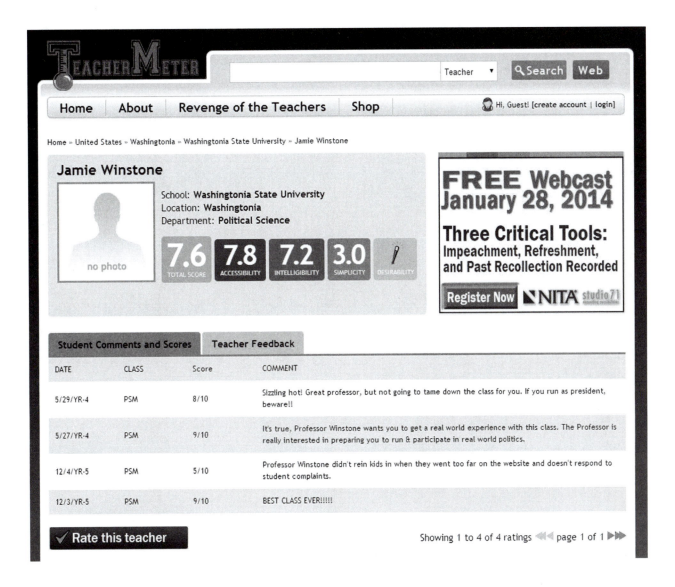

*Simplicity - How simple is it to get a good grade in this class?

1	2	3	4	5	6	7	8	9	10
Tough									Simple

*Accessibility - How helpful and accessible is the teacher outside the classroom?

1	2	3	4	5	6	7	8	9	10
Impossible									Helpful

*Intelligibility - How were the teacher's methods and course materials?

1	2	3	4	5	6	7	8	9	10
Worthless									Fantastic

*Interest level prior to enrolling in the course

1	2	3	4	5	6	7	8	9	10
Not Interested									Hot Hot Hot

*Course Materials - Were they appropriate for the class?

1	2	3	4	5	6	7	8	9	10
Inappropriate									Appropriate

*Desirability - How good looking is this teacher?

1	2	3	4	5	6	7	8	9	10
Not									Hot

Exhibit 14

Anonymous Email to Dean Dylan Jeffries

From: anonymous@hotmail.nita
To: djefferies@washingtonia.nita
Subject: Anonymous Tip
Date: October 31, YR-3 2:10 p.m.

Dear Dean Jeffries,

Attached is a video I stumbled upon of Washingtonia University student, Riley Evans, drinking while underage at a party. Additionally, I have attached a screenshot of a post on Professor Winstone's Politics & Social Media Class Facebook alleging that Evans is not the original author of the work Evans submits for grades.

As a student who values the integrity of this university, I couldn't, in good conscience, allow Evan's actions go unpunished, which is why I am forwarding this to you anonymously.

-Annon

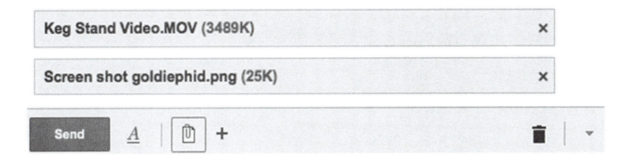

Goldiephd
Hey. I am a law student at Washingtonia College of Law (WCL)...just wanted to share my two cents.
Evans paid me to write freshman essays last year...I totally believe the cheating stories.
Like   **Comment**   October 31, YR-3 at 12:04pm

EvansYR-3 did you send this to this disciplinary board? How dare you?
Like   November 1, YR-3 at 12:35pm

Mritch4prez Goldie doesn't need to! Everyone knows you're a cheat and a liar!
Like   November 1, YR-3 at 12:40pm

Write a comment...

STATE OF WASHINGTONIA SCHOOL CYBERBULLYING PROTECTION ACT OF YR-6

(a)   Each school within the Washingtonia state school system, including primary, secondary, collegiate, and charter schools, shall develop a policy to prohibit and punish cyberbullying to foster the learning environment required of a state-funded school system.

(1)   "Cyberbullying" is the repeated use by one or more students of a verbal, written, or electronic expression, or any combination thereof, directed at the victim that creates a hostile environment for the victim or interferes with the victim's rights at school.

(A)   "Technology" includes, but is not limited to, telephones, computers, game consoles, and personal electronic devices such as MP3 music players, computer tablets, and smartphones.

(B)   "Electronic communications" include, but are not limited to, any written, oral, or visual imagery sent through technology included in (A) above. Examples of communications include websites, electronic mail, instant messages, and postings to social media or shared media sites, either within the school's domain or in the public domain through use of the school's equipment.

(C)   A "hostile environment" is a situation that is permeated with intimidation, ridicule, or insult that is sufficiently severe or pervasive to substantially interfere with the victim's educational performance, opportunities, or benefits.

(b)   Each policy shall be distributed at least annually to all students, faculty members, and employees of the school system. Distribution may be in printed or electronic form.

(c)   School employees, faculty, or students who comply in good faith with the procedures set forth in this act are immune from causes of action arising from incidents prohibited under this act.

(d)   The First Amendment right to free speech is not a defense to any claim brought pursuant to the Cyberbullying Protection Act of YR-6.

JURY INSTRUCTIONS

PRELIMINARY JURY INSTRUCTIONS

You have now been sworn as the jury to try this case. This is a civil case involving disputed claims between the parties. Those claims and other matters will be explained to you later. By your verdict, you will decide the disputed issues of fact. I will decide the questions of law that arise during the trial, and before you retire to deliberate at the close of the trial, I will instruct you on the law that you are to follow and apply in reaching your verdict. It is your responsibility to determine the facts and to apply the law to those facts. Thus, the function of the jury and the function of the judge are well defined, and they do not overlap. This is one of the fundamental principles of our system of justice.

Before proceeding further, it will be helpful for you to understand how a trial is conducted. In a few moments, the attorneys for the parties will have an opportunity to make opening statements, in which they may explain to you the issues in the case and summarize the facts that they expect the evidence will show. Following the opening statements, witnesses will be called to testify under oath. They will be examined and cross-examined by the attorneys. Documents and other exhibits also may be received as evidence.

After all the evidence has been received, the attorneys will again have the opportunity to address you and to make their final arguments. The statements that the attorneys now make and the arguments that they later make are not to be considered by you either as evidence in the case or as your instruction on the law. Nevertheless, these statements and arguments are intended to help you properly understand the issues, the evidence, and the applicable law, so you should give them your close attention. Following the final arguments by the attorneys, I will instruct you on the law.

You should give careful attention to the testimony and other evidence as it is received and presented for your consideration, but you should not form or express any opinion about the case until you have received all the evidence, the arguments of the attorneys, and the instructions on the law from me. In other words, you should not form or express any opinion about the case until you retire to the jury room to consider your verdict.

The attorneys are trained in the rules of evidence and trial procedure, and it is their duty to make all objections they feel are proper. When a lawyer makes an objection, I will either overrule or sustain the objection. If I overruled an objection to a question, the witness will answer the question. If I sustain an objection, the witness will not answer, but you must not speculate on what might have happened or what the witness might have said had I permitted the witness to answer the question. You should not draw any inference from the question itself.

During the trial, it may be necessary for me to confer with the attorneys out of your hearing, talking about matters of law and other matters that require consideration by me alone. It is impossible for me to predict when such a conference may be required or how long it will last. When such conferences occur, they will be conducted so as to consume as little of your time as necessary for a fair and orderly trial of the case.

At this time, the attorneys for the parties will have an opportunity to make their opening statements.

FINAL JURY INSTRUCTIONS

Members of the jury, I shall now instruct you on the law that you must follow in reaching your verdict. It is your duty as jurors to decide the issues, and only those issues, that I submit for determination by your verdict. In reaching your verdict, you should consider and weigh the evidence, decide the disputed issues of fact, and apply the law on which I shall instruct you to the facts as you find them, from the evidence.

The evidence in this case consists of the sworn testimony of the witnesses, all exhibits received into evidence, and all facts that may be admitted or agreed to by the parties. In determining the facts, you may draw reasonable inferences from the evidence. You may make deductions and reach conclusions that reason and common sense lead you to draw from the facts shown by the evidence in this case, but you should not speculate on any matters outside the evidence.

In determining the believability of any witness and the weight to be given the testimony of any witness, you may properly consider the demeanor of the witness while testifying; the frankness or lack of frankness of the witness; the intelligence of the witness; any interest the witness may have in the outcome of the case; the means and opportunity the witness had to know the facts about which the witness testified; the ability of the witness to remember the matters about which the witness testified; and the reasonableness of the testimony of the witness, considered in the light of the all the evidence in the case and in light of your own experience and common sense.

The issue for your determination on the claim of Riley Evans is whether Washingtonia State University was negligent in failing to take meaningful measures to prevent the ongoing cyberbullying against Riley Evans, and, if so, whether such negligence was the proximate cause of any damages to Evans. In order to establish negligence on the part of the Washingtonia State University, Riley Evans had to prove that:

The Washingtonia State University had a duty to Riley Evans to provide a safe school environment;

Riley Evans was, in fact, bullied or harassed by one or more students at the Washingtonia State University;

The Washingtonia State University knew of bullying or harassment by one or more students towards Riley Evans;

After learning of the bullying or harassment, it was foreseeable that the bullying or harassment would continue;

Such harassment or bullying did continue; and

The Washingtonia State University did not take reasonable steps to prevent the injury or damage caused by the bullying student or students to Riley Evans.

The Washingtonia State University is a quasi-municipal corporation. Under the law of this jurisdiction, employees such as adjunct faculty members, faculty members, and deans of the university are agents of the Washingtonia State University. The University is liable if its agents act negligently as it relates to the role of their employment.

Whether Riley Evans was in fact bullied or harassed is to be determined using a reasonable person, or objective standard. That is, the question for your determination is not whether Riley Evans subjectively believed to be bullied and/or harassed, but what a reasonable person would believe.

The Washingtonia State University has asserted what is called an affirmative defense of assumption of the risk. In order to establish Riley Evans assumed the risk, the Washingtonia State University had to establish Riley Evans had knowledge of a risk or danger, appreciated such risk or danger, and yet voluntarily placed himself [or herself] in the environment. The knowledge required is actual knowledge. The standard to be applied is a subjective one, of what Riley Evans saw, knew, understood, and appreciated. It is not actual knowledge where it merely appears that Riley Evans should or could have discovered the danger. An individual assumes all the ordinary risks of his or her voluntary acts or the environment in which he or she voluntarily places himself or herself. An individual does not, however, assume obscure and unknown risks, which are not naturally incident to such acts or environment and which, in the existing conditions, would not be reasonably observed and appreciated. However, if fully informed, Riley Evans may be deemed to assume the risk even though the dangerous condition was caused by the negligence of the Washingtonia State University. Should you find the Washingtonia State University proved Riley Evans assumed the risk by a preponderance of the evidence, then you must find in favor of Washingtonia State University.

Shortly, you will retire to the jury room and be given a verdict form to fill out. Answer yes or no to all questions unless otherwise instructed. A yes answer must be based on a preponderance of the evidence unless you are otherwise instructed. If you do not find that a preponderance of the evidence supports a yes answer, then answer no. The term "preponderance of the evidence" means the greater weight and degree of credible evidence admitted in this case. Whenever a question requires an answer other than yes or no, your answer must be based on a preponderance of the evidence unless you are otherwise instructed.

At this point in the trial, you, as jurors, are deciding only if the Washingtonia State University was negligent or whether Riley Evans assumed the risk. You will first return a verdict on that issue. If you find that the Washingtonia State University was negligent, you will hear additional argument from the attorneys and you will hear additional witnesses testify concerning damages.

Your verdict must be based on the evidence that has been received and the law on which I have instructed you. In reaching your verdict, you are not to be swayed from the performance of your duty by prejudice, sympathy, or any other sentiment for or against any party.

When you retire to the jury room, you should select one of your members to act as foreperson to preside over your deliberations and sign your verdict. Your verdict must be unanimous—that is, your verdict must be agreed to by each of you. You will be given a verdict form, which I shall now read and explain to you.

(READ VERDICT FORM)

When you have agreed on your verdict, the foreperson, acting for the jury, should date and sign the verdict form and return it to the courtroom. You may not retire to consider your verdict.

IN THE COURT OF WASHINGTONIA — CIVIL DIVISION

RILEY EVANS   :   No. 123-YR-2

v.   :

WASHINGTONIA STATE UNIVERSITY   :

VERDICT FORM

We, the jury, return the following verdict:

1. Was there negligence on the part of Washingtonia State University in failing to take measures to prevent cyberbullying against Riley Evans, which was a legal cause of damage to Riley Evans?

    YES_____   NO_____

If your answer to question 1 is NO, you should not proceed further except to date and sign this verdict form and return it to the courtroom. If your answer to question 1 is YES, please answer question 2.

2. Did Riley Evans assume the risk of injury he [or she] sustained?

    YES_____   NO_____

If your answer to question 2 is YES, you should not proceed further except to date and sign this verdict form and return it to the courtroom. If your answer to question 2 is NO, please answer question 3.

3. Please state the percentage of fault, if any, which was the legal cause of Riley Evan's injury that you charge to:

    Washingtonia State University   _____%

    Riley Evans   _____%

The total of the two percentages must equal 100 percent.

SO SAY WE ALL this _____ day of _____, YR-2.

                                    _____
                                    Foreperson